Mellowing MANDALAS #1
ADULT COLORING BOOK

42 All-New, Custom-drawn Mandala Designs for Your Coloring Delight

COLORING WITH JOY PUBLISHING

COLORING
WITH
JOY
PUBLISHING

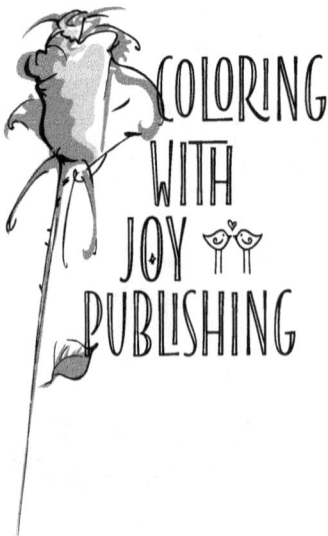

Book and Cover Design: Joy Rose
Mandala Cover Design, *Sid Ork,* for Coloring With Joy Publishing

ISBN: 978-0-9978133-2-6
Published and created in the United States of America
Printed in the United States of America

Title Page image available for coloring on page 83.

To my coloring friends:

Are you ready for some color? I don't know about you, but for me, a little doodling and coloring goes a long way toward reducing stress. We're delighted to bring you a new adult coloring book for your fun and relaxation. We listened to your comments around the web and the world of adult stress-reduction coloring. That means we've included a great mix of brand-new, custom-drawn mandalas in this collection of **42 designs on more than 90 pages.**

Some of the designs are quite complex and others are very simple. The variety gives you *wonderful* choices, allowing you to pick what you want based on your mood or just how much time you have to yourself. We've even included one or two for the younger members of your household, to keep them busy while you're relaxing with more compex creations. Some of the designs are *fierce* and some are whimsical.

Page numbers are displayed in a light grey, on the back of each drawing page, only. To make it easy for you to find where you left off.

Each image is backed with a blank page. Two extra blank pages are included at the back, for you to cut out and place between your book pages while you are coloring, to protect against any bleed-through.

We love to hear feedback and suggestions. Please see page 89 to find our Contact email address. Don't hesitate to write me!

We hope that you'll love our latest coloring extravaganza, and that you'll have fun and relax when *Coloring With Joy.*

Have a blast!

JOY ROSE

8

14

16

18

28

30

34

48

50

52

DEAR FELLOW ARTIST,

I hope that you've enjoyed the wonders of coloring our gorgeous, custom-drawn mandalas for stress reduction. I also hope that you've had as much fun coloring in these drawings as I had in putting this book together. Please look for other books in the Joy Rose *Coloring With Joy* series of adult coloring books. If you have comments, or suggestions, please email me at:

COLORINGWITHJOYPUBLISHING@GMAIL.COM

I'd love to hear from you. We're always looking for your input. Your ideas, what you like to color. Was this book easy enough? Hard enough? Do you want more mandalas like page 82? Page 46? Let us know. We are creating new books and new designs constantly--for *you*. Look for *Books 2* and *3* of **Mellowing Mandalas,** which should be in bookstores now.

COLOR WITH JOY,

Joy Rose

Page Intentionally Left Blank For Your Use

Page Intentional-
ly Left Blank For
Your Use

www.ingramcontent.com/pod-product-compliance
Lightning Source LLC
Chambersburg PA
CBHW080525030426
42337CB00023B/4633